YOLT

(You Only Live Twice)

YOLT

(You Only Live Twice)

Thinking Ahead to the Next Life
by Looking at Life Today

Cindi Jasa

YOLT

For publishing inquiries, contact:
YOLT Publishing
c/o CMI
13518 L Street
Omaha, NE 68137

ISBN: 978-0-9982931-2-7

Publishing and production services by Concierge Marketing Inc.

Library of Congress and Cataloging-in-Publication
data on file with the publisher

Printed in the USA
10 9 8 7 6 5 4

I want to say a huge 'thanks' to my friends and family members who believed in me enough to take time to read and offer your suggestions on this project (some of you more than once!), and to help and encourage me in this dream of mine!!

You will never know how much that means to me! I love you all!!

Introduction

My pastor, Les Beauchamp, made a comment in one of his sermons that caught my attention. He said that we only live twice. It had been on my heart to write a book for quite awhile, so when I heard that, I decided it would be a great place to start (and also a really good book title).

I think all of us have heard it said "You Only Live Once" (YOLO), but when you think about it, that isn't really true. The truth is, "**You Only Live Twice**" (hence the "**YOLT**") and the way in which you live the first life has everything to do with what the second one has in store for you.

My intention in this small booklet isn't to give you all the theological reasons for anything, but to give you some food for thought that will hopefully open your eyes to see that your life on this earth matters not only here and now, but for all of eternity.

I have kept it short because of all the people I know who say "I don't have time" or "I don't like to read". My prayer is that you will take the time to read and consider what is in this booklet. Many don't yet know God or understand what He is about. Others may have encountered Him and chosen to go another way. There are also those who love God wholeheartedly. Wherever you fall in the spectrum, I hope to encourage you in your life's journey.

"Friends, please take what I've written most seriously. I've kept this as brief as possible; I haven't piled on a lot of extras."

Hebrews 13:22

YOLT

You only live twice. That doesn't even sound right. We have been told that you only live once and so you need to go for all the gusto and live your life to the fullest.

So what does that mean for you? What would a full life look like from your perspective? Does it include making lots of money, owning the most and the best "stuff", having a prestigious career or being in relationship with people you consider important (or better yet, feeling like you are that important person)? Would it be traveling the world and experiencing exciting adventures? Maybe for you it's getting married and having a family.

We all have a different idea of what a full life would be. I would guess that it's what we invest most of our time, thoughts and money in and what we put our hope in. I believe many people are so concerned with getting through their "bucket list" that they are missing the purpose they were created for.

Fulfilling God's purpose for you is the most exciting thing you could ever do. It brings joy and a sense that your life matters because you are making a difference not only on this earth (the first life), but also in heaven (the second life). When many people think of what God has for them, they think that it must be something unexciting and probably involves being a missionary in Africa or some remote place for the rest of their lives. God has a special purpose for each one of us right where we are. And I guarantee that if you are one who is chosen to go to Africa, it will be the most exciting adventure of your life!

Have you ever seen the round toy with different shapes cut out into it and you have to put the correct shape in the corresponding hole? Did you know that you have a 'hole' in you that can only be filled with God? When we don't understand this, we try to put our desires and our goals in that slot (possessions, money, fame, etc.) and then we can't figure out why they don't bring us the fulfillment we had hoped for. We still feel empty inside.

What is your purpose for being here? Have you ever really taken time to stop and think about that question? We tend to get so caught up in the busyness of life that we don't think about why we are even here in the first place.

To really understand life, we would need to go all the way back in time, even before this world was created. It all started with God because He has always existed. It's hard for us to comprehend how someone could exist without being created but that's one of those things we will never be able to wrap our minds around.

God (the Father), Jesus (the Son) and Holy Spirit (the Spirit of God) lived in heaven with the angels and life was perfect. They needed nothing or no one to make them complete. But God wanted to give His Son, Jesus, a family. That's where mankind enters the picture.

The problem was that heaven is a perfect place and no sin or evil can enter there. God already knew before creating man that he would sin and not be able to get into heaven on his own. Because of God's justice, a price had to be paid for our sins. So He came up with a solution to the problem before we were ever

born. That solution would cost Jesus (and God the Father) everything, but it was the only solution that would be sufficient.

God the Father presented the plan to Jesus, His Son. He told Jesus that because He loved Him so much, He wanted to give Him a family who would love Him forever. But for that to happen, Jesus would have to be willing to give up the power and authority that He had in heaven and come to earth as a baby – completely human. He would have to live a sinless life and then die a horrible death at the hands of the very ones He would create.

As if that wasn't enough, Jesus would also have to endure the full wrath of God's punishment for our sins while He hung on the cross. The wrath wasn't because God is angry or vengeful, but because He is loving and pure, and heaven is a perfect place where sin can't enter.

After contemplating the plan, Jesus agreed to it because He already saw us before we were ever born and He loved us enough to die for us. The purpose was, if we accepted the plan and the provision, we would be adopted into the family of God.

So how does that happen? How do we become part of God's family? Jesus did the part that we couldn't do. He lived a sinless life and offered His blood as the sacrifice for our sins that would ultimately keep us out of heaven. The part that so often trips us up is that we have to receive the gift that is offered to us – the gift of forgiveness and a new life lived out with a new purpose.

When we were created we were given a free will. That means we get to make our own choices in life. Without that, we would never be free to choose or reject the love that God offers. He doesn't force His love and His way on us or demand that we love Him back because that wouldn't be real love. Real love is a choice.

God asks you to accept the free gift He offers you. You may struggle because you don't really understand what that means. You may think you have to do something to earn God's love.

I think the hardest part for us is that it seems too easy, but we are told to come like a child. I'm guessing that's because children don't try to complicate things. They are trusting, open and eager to learn.

"Unless you turn to God from your sins and become as little children, you will never get into the Kingdom of Heaven."

Matthew 18:3

We often think we have to "clean ourselves up" on our own before God would ever accept us. The truth is we can't make lasting changes without His help.

But we still have the problem of our free will. Too many times we choose without knowing the full picture. If you take time to really think about all that Jesus did for you and just how much He loves you, why would you be afraid to trust Him with your life? He willingly gave His life for you.

God knows everything about you – from before you were even born until you will take your last breath. He saw you being formed in your mother's womb

(Psalm 139)

He has seen every joy and every pain that you have walked and will walk through in your whole life. He knows everything from the number of hairs on your head to how many days you have left on this earth.

At times you may feel like God has abandoned you but the truth is, He has been there at every turn. And most importantly, He has never turned His back on you. He has loved you the same through your highest and your lowest moments.

Jesus was abandoned by God on the cross so that even in the midst of our suffering and our rebellion, we would never be forsaken or abandoned by God. We have blamed God for not caring, which is far from the truth.

"For God so loved the world that He gave His One and only Son, that whoever believes in Him shall not perish but have eternal life. For God did not send His Son into the world to condemn the world, but that the world through Him might be saved."

John 3:16-17

God has bigger purposes in allowing us to suffer… bigger than just our comfort. He allows us to suffer because we change through suffering. We grow up. We hurt with others better, we become humble, but mostly, we want and need Him more when we suffer.

We have been given the greatest example of how to suffer well through Jesus' life.

"Though He was God's Son, He learned trusting-obedience by what He suffered, just as we do."

Hebrews 5:8

Suffering was a big part of Jesus' life and it will be part of our lives too. Everyone has struggles, but if you know Jesus, He offers comfort and help in your times of trouble.

Do you believe God made you the way you are for a reason? Can you believe He put you where you are because, in His wisdom, He knew that was the best place for you? Consider the family He lovingly placed you in…your parents, your siblings (or lack of). Do you dare trust that God knew what He was doing when He created you? Can you go a step further and believe that He did it all for your good? Would you be willing to even thank Him for every part of your life?

God has a perfect plan for your life, but He can't move you to the next step until you joyfully accept your present situation as part of that plan. What happens next is God's move, not yours.

Maybe your life hasn't gone as you would have hoped. Maybe you have had more than your share of heartache. I have no idea why some people seem to have a much easier life than others but I do know that if God gave us the life we really think we want, we would probably never need Him. That's because most of us would choose the easy path.

When hard things come into our lives, I believe that God, in His mercy, uses those trials (if we let Him) to allow us to consider Him and His great love for us. He didn't cause them to happen (we live in a sinful, broken world), but His desire is to use them to save us from ourselves.

He may be using people who irritate you to show you areas in your life where you still need to trust Him and learn how to love better. We encounter situations daily that could easily frustrate or anger us but what if we believed that nothing happens to us that God doesn't allow for our ultimate good – that He is using each thing to make us more like Himself (patient, loving, kind, etc.)?

God's purpose in our trials is to refine our character. He is much more concerned with our character than He is our comfort. Life wasn't meant to be easy. We too easily become like spoiled children when we expect life to go our way. God's way is always the better way.

Many of us have heard the story of Jesus so many times that it has become just another story that we tend to take for granted. Or we may think that it's just a story and it really isn't true. As for me, I would stake my life on it. If for any reason I'm wrong, so be it. I would rather live my life with

Jesus because I can't even imagine how I would have made it this far without Him!

I love the song "Through All of It" by Colton Dixon. In it he says; "Life's been a journey. I've seen joy, I've seen regret. But You have been my God through all of it."

God has been with me through all of my ups and downs. I would never have made it on my own. He gives me hope and strength when I am overwhelmed by life. He shares my joys and my sorrows. He delights me with His love. He is my reason to keep moving forward each and every day. I know that heaven will be my home one day!

Even as I am writing this, I feel like I am speaking to myself. I still have so far to go but I know that God loves me enough to continue working in me to make me all that has He planned for me to be.

> "I don't mean to say I am perfect (complete).
> I haven't learned all I should even yet, but
> I keep working toward that day when I will
> finally be all that Christ saved me for and
> wants me to be."
>
> Philippians 3:12

In Control or Sovereign?

I used to believe that God was in control of all that goes on in this world. It left me feeling powerless and like my prayers really didn't matter because I couldn't change anything anyway. I realized that if God was in control we would just be like puppets that were used to accomplish His purposes. But that wasn't His plan.

Of course God could definitely do away with all the evil and injustice in the world if He wanted to, but it would mean taking away our free will (or He could just eliminate the human race). But He loves us too much to do that.

God isn't in control but He is sovereign. In that sovereignty He chooses to invade human life by affecting our circumstances and experiences without violating our free will. God doesn't force or manipulate us so He can control us. Instead He governs us by offering choices with consequences. If you are a parent, you may use the same type of method.

> "Don't be angry when the Lord punishes you. Don't be discouraged when He has to show you where you are wrong. For when He punishes you, it proves that He loves you. God's correction is always right and for our best good, that we may share His holiness."

Hebrews 12:5-6, 10

The reason God is working to make us more like Himself is because Jesus is coming back to earth one more time. His second coming will be much different than His first coming. Jesus will come in power and authority and He will gather up all those who truly love Him and have made the decision to follow Him. I believe His second coming will take many by surprise because they aren't prepared or even expecting it. But Jesus is coming back (maybe even sooner than we might think) and we need to be ready for that amazing day!

Becoming Like Jesus

Jesus showed us how much He loves us by dying for us so we could live with Him forever in heaven. He asks us to love Him in return but also to love others – especially those who are the hardest to love. He died for everyone – not just those we think of as "good" or those who are easy to love (anyone can do that). Love is the crowning feature of anyone who truly follows God.

When you invite Jesus into your life, His love becomes a part of you but you still have to choose to live that love out in your daily life. Love doesn't just happen. It's a choice. It involves partnering with

God's Spirit who lives inside of you, allowing Him to teach you how to love others in the same way God loves you.

> "If anyone boasts, 'I love God', and goes right on hating his brother or sister, thinking nothing of it, he is a liar. If he won't love the person he can see, how can he love the God he can't see? Loving God includes loving people. You've got to love both."
>
> I John 4:20-21

Without love and unity in our families, our churches and among people in general, Christians look just like those in the world around them. We are called to love and even pray for those who mistreat us.

If we love God and love people, forgiveness will flow freely from us to others. How could we not forgive when we have been forgiven so much? It's hard to remember when people hurt us that they are the ones who are probably hurting the most (hurting people hurt people). What if we asked God to help us see others through His eyes instead of only seeing what they have done to us? Maybe our love could help them find God's love.

As humans we tend to categorize sin. When you think of sin, what comes to mind? Is it theft, murder, or something worse than that? So where do anger, lies, ungratefulness, selfishness, gossip, unforgiveness and the many other things we consider "lesser sins" (or we don't even think about them as being wrong) come in? We don't understand that sin is sin. There aren't "degrees of sin".

If we say we hate someone (or even call them a fool), it's the same as murder. If we think wrong thoughts or look upon someone with lust in our heart, we have already committed adultery.

> "And the person who keeps every law of God, but makes one little slip, is just as guilty as the person who has broken every law there is."

James 2:10

That sounds pretty harsh, but Jesus would have had to die even if all you ever did was tell a lie.

If we really saw people as Jesus did, we would do what He did. Instead of judging them, He looked past their mistakes and failures and reached out to them in love. Jesus came to save sinners, not righteous people. It's the sick who need a doctor. If we turn our backs on others because we

consider their sin to be greater than ours, we have set ourselves up as the Judge (God), and that's not a good place to be. The problem is, we can't see people's hearts, but God can.

When we see what Jesus went through to demonstrate His love for us, His request doesn't seem that unreasonable. He loved us when we were unlovable and He paid for our sins before we even asked Him to forgive us. We are asked to do the same for others. Jesus even goes so far as to say:

"For if you forgive men when they sin against you, your heavenly Father will also forgive you. But if you do not forgive men their sins, your Father will not forgive your sins."

Matthew 6:14-15

Our unforgiveness blocks God's blessings and forgiveness in our lives. Refusing to forgive is like drinking poison and hoping the other person dies. It can destroy you and not even affect them. God forgives us the minute we confess our sins to Him. But if we only want forgiveness for ourselves and refuse to forgive others who have hurt us, we will suffer. Our peace, joy and even our health will be affected because that's how we were made. God calls us to forgive.

"So be careful how you act; these are difficult days. Don't be fools; be wise: make the most of every opportunity you have for doing good. Don't act thoughtlessly, but try to find out and do whatever the Lord wants you to do."

Ephesians 5:15-17

Many people think they can live the Christian life without Jesus and without His Word (the Bible). They "believe" in God (so does the devil – so much that he trembles!) and hope that will be enough to buy them a ticket to heaven. That would be like going to school and not opening the textbooks, hoping you learned enough in the discussions (church) to pass the tests. I don't think you would hear the teacher (God the Father) say "Well done". It's hard to know what is asked of you when you never took the time to ask questions in order to learn why you were in the class to begin with.

The Bible is God's love letter to you. That's a really good place to learn about His character, His love, and His purposes for you. God's Word is one of the main ways He speaks to you. Through it, He gives encouragement for the journey you are on. It can teach and correct you in a loving way if you read and then obey what it says.

Prayer is another way to hear God speak to you. Prayer is simply talking to God, just like you would to a friend. He wants more of a relationship than for us to just come and ask for His blessings. He wants us to share our hearts and every part of our lives with Him. When we take time to pray and sit quietly in God's presence, He reveals His heart to us. He even considers us His friends!

Did you know that God loves your prayers? So many times I feel like my prayers are inadequate, but God doesn't see them that way. He loves it when we take time throughout our day to talk to Him and ask for His wisdom and direction. His desire is that we speak to Him all day long and share the good and the hard things we encounter. If we want prayer to impact our lives, we need to speak and listen. God speaks to us all the time but we have to be listening if we want to hear His voice.

Did you know that our prayers affect history? They make a difference in our lives and in the lives of those we pray for. God acts in response to our (your) prayers! When we pray, our prayers set God's answers in motion. That's amazing to me! Our prayers not only reach God, but they touch His heart.

Our words have much more power than we realize. Did you know that Jesus spoke and the world was created (Genesis 1)? Everything He did was accomplished through His spoken word. As you read the Bible and words jump out at you, God wants you to speak those things over your life and the lives of others.

Our words have great impact on us and on those we speak about. "What you say is what you get." The Bible even goes so far as to say that life and death are in the power of the tongue. That's a pretty strong statement!

If we really took time to listen to what comes out of our mouths, I think we would be shocked. When you speak the name of God or Jesus, does it please Him or break His heart? I am sure that when God's name is used as a curse instead of a blessing, His heart hurts. I know mine does.

How do you talk about yourself? Did you know that God has purposes designed just for you? Do you see yourself as the one-of-a-kind creation that God made you to be or do you speak mostly of your failures and shortcomings? God has labeled you "Chosen, Loved and His unique creation". How have you labeled yourself?

What words come out of your mouth when things aren't going your way? Try thanking God for every situation and person that comes into your life. Maybe

the very thing that causes you stress is a test to see what is really in your heart.

Consider this statement in Matthew 12:36:

"Every one of these careless words is going to come back to haunt you. There will be a time of reckoning. Words are powerful; take them seriously."

We will have to give an account of every word we have ever spoken. We need to stop and think before we speak!

God is good all the time and He's in a good mood! That's His nature even when we don't always see Him that way. We can trust Him with every part of our lives. God doesn't put our lives on an eternal scale to see if our good deeds outweigh our bad deeds. Remember, He loves us just the way we are. But when we think about how loved we are, it should cause us to want to please and obey God by loving ourselves and others the way He does.

If we truly understood how short this life is and believed that all of our choices have eternal consequences, I believe we would want to know how to live a life that matters, not only here and now but forever. If you compare the length of your life to eternity (no beginning and no end), it's less than a second of time. Even if we lived to be 100 years old, that would still be just a moment.

Have you ever heard the saying that the years of your life are expressed by the date you were born, followed by the date you died? What matters is how you spend the "dash" between those two dates. What legacy do you want to leave to your loved ones? Is it just about an inheritance of money and things or are you leaving them an example that is worthy of following?

When I attend a funeral, I always have lots of questions going through my head. What do people believe they have to do to get to heaven? Have they been told that going to church regularly will get them there? Do they think that baptism is the key? Do they think they have to do (or not do) certain things to be good enough to get there? Do they believe others can stand in the gap and pray them into heaven (either before or after they die)?

Jesus didn't die on the cross so we would attend church, keep a list of rules, and do our best to be good enough to hopefully get into heaven. If that's all it would take, He wouldn't have had to die.

Each of us must give an account of our lives to God.

"For we must all appear before the judgment
seat of Christ, that each one may be
recompensed for his deeds in the body,
according to what he has done, whether
good or bad." We are only responsible for
ourselves and our choices.

2 Corinthians 5:10

A well loved and respected couple in our city just recently died in a horrible car crash. Even though it was a tragedy for the city and beyond, they loved Jesus and spent their lives serving Him. He had just given a talk to some school children that morning about being sold out for Jesus. He asked them the question, "If you were to die today, do you know where you would spend eternity?"

Part of the scripture he used was in
Philippians 1:20-21 where it says,

". . that now as always Christ will be exalted
in my body, whether by life or by death. For
to me, to live is Christ and to die is gain."

He knew that dead or alive, he couldn't lose! His life had a huge impact on many and I am certain that God, in His sovereignty, will also cause that same life to continue to have a lasting impact on those he touched during his lifetime.

Their untimely death made me stop and think about my own life and consider what kind of an impact I am making in the lives of those around me. How many people will be in heaven because of my life? That's a pretty sobering thought.

I don't want to stand before God on that day with my completed bucket list. I'm pretty sure He wouldn't be too impressed with that. My ultimate goal is to fulfill the purposes He has planned for me for this first life. Then my reward will be great in the second one (the one that lasts for eternity!).

What are you living your life for? Are you living for yourself or for Jesus? All that we have comes from God and it all belongs to Him. It's ours to use and to share until we leave this earth. Have you ever thought about the fact that God doesn't bless (prosper) you just so you can have more for yourself? He does it so you can help others in their need. We can't take any of our worldly goods with us when we die, but we can send our treasures on ahead by making an eternal impact in the lives of others now, in this first life.

We can't buy our way into Heaven, but we can invest in eternity by sharing Jesus and what we have been given with others. And then we get to spend all of eternity with the people we influenced on this earth. Now that's good news! God has promised that

we can never out give Him. I can personally testify to that truth. He always wins the challenge!

Only what we do for God lasts for eternity. Everything else is wasted. Every movement we make in response to God has a ripple effect, touching family, neighbors, friends and community. If we believe in God it should alter our language. If we love God it should affect our daily relationships. If we have faith in God, hope should enter into our lives and overflow into our homes, our work places and everywhere we go.

You can't control the length of your life, but you can control the depth of it. You can make a difference in this world now, while you still have breath. It doesn't matter how young or how old you are. God can use you if you let Him.

Do you want your life to count for eternity or just be content to pursue the "American Dream"? Don't waste any more of your life. Focus your energy on the one thing that matters, Jesus Christ and the cross, and be willing to die for it. Following Jesus isn't easy, but I can tell you from experience that it's worth it!

Conclusion

Now you get to decide what you will do with what you have just read. This is the greatest love story of all time. It's the story of a Father's love for His Son and the Son's love and desire for a family. It's about preparing ourselves for the return of Jesus with the help of God's own Spirit who lives in those who put their faith, hope and trust in Him.

You may think that you're a pretty good person (maybe even a really good one). We like to play the 'comparison game' where we measure our lives against those we think of as really bad so we come out looking good. We keep God at a distance. But we

can't be forgiven if we don't think we've done anything wrong. If we had never sinned, Jesus would not have had to die to take our punishment.

God gave us the 10 commandments to diagnose our condition. He didn't give them to make sure we would never enjoy this life. Actually, it's just the opposite. He gave them as safeguards, to make our lives better, and to protect us from things He knew would ultimately harm us and steal our joy.

Paul writes in Romans 4:5:

"For being saved is a gift; if a person could earn it by being good, then it wouldn't be free – but it is! It is given to those who do not work for it. God declares sinners to be good in His sight if they have faith in Christ to save them from God's wrath."

That's really good news! You are loved more than you know and you can be declared good in God's sight by receiving His gift of salvation and forgiveness. Jesus died on the cross with YOU in mind! You can either fully receive the free gift Jesus offers or you choose to miss it. Salvation didn't cost us anything, but it cost God everything!! God doesn't send anyone to hell. We make that choice ourselves by ignoring or refusing the gift that Jesus died to give us and we miss out on eternity with God because of that choice.

Do you just believe there is a God or do you know God? Do you acknowledge what He did for you on the cross but you haven't let it change the way you live? It's not just about saying a prayer and going on with life as usual. True salvation requires repentance. That means you are truly sorry for your sins and you ask God to live in you and to help you change the way you have been living.

Have you fully surrendered your life to Him and asked Him to be the Lord (the One in control) of your life? Salvation is so much more than just missing hell and going to heaven. It affects us right now by bringing fullness to every day of this first life we've been given, and it takes us safely into eternity (the second life).

When you stand before God on that great day, He will ask, "What did you do with my Son, Jesus Christ?" and "What did you do with what I gave you?" The first question will determine where you spend eternity. The second question will determine your reward in heaven.

The answers to both those questions can be found in God's Word, the Bible. It's an open book test because God's desire is that we don't fail because of ignorance. But we do have to open the Book. In it God has provided all that we need for life and godliness.

So how do you make the choice to take Jesus as your Savior? It's as simple as saying a prayer like this:

"Lord Jesus, I'm so sorry for my sins that sent you to the cross. Thank you for dying in my place. I don't want to take your sacrifice for granted. Please use me right now and for the rest of my life on this earth to bring glory to You, the Son of God. Use all that You have given me to reach others for you. Help me to be ready for Your return. I love you Jesus. Amen."

But don't just stop with a prayer. Remember, you only live twice (**YOLT**). The life you live here on earth is the one that determines the life you will live for eternity. That's a really long time! My prayer is that this booklet has caused you to think about your choices and what eternity holds for you. I look forward to heaven and I can only imagine how incredible it will be to spend forever with all those who put their trust in Jesus!! I pray that I will see you there!

And now, "I ask God, the glorious Father of our Lord Jesus Christ, to give you wisdom to see clearly and really understand who Christ is and all that He has done for you. I pray that your hearts will be flooded with light so that you can see something of the future He has called you to share. I want you to realize that God has been made rich because we who are Christ's have been given to Him!"

Ephesians 1:17-18

Psalm 139:1-18

"O Lord, You have examined my heart and know everything about me. You know when I sit or stand. When far away, You know my every thought. You chart the path ahead of me, and tell me where to stop and rest. Every moment, You know where I am. You know what I am going to say before I even say it. You both precede and follow me, and place Your hand of blessing on my head.

This is too glorious, too wonderful to believe! I can never be lost to Your Spirit! I can never get away from my God! If I go up to heaven, You are there: if I go down to the place of the dead, You are there. If I ride

the morning winds to the farthest oceans, even there Your hand will guide me, Your strength will support me. If I try to hide in the darkness, the night becomes light around me. For even darkness cannot hide from God; to You the night shines as bright as day. Darkness and light are both alike to You.

You made all the delicate, inner parts of my body, and knit them together in my mother's womb. Thank You for making me so wonderfully complex! It is amazing to think about. Your workmanship is marvelous- and how well I know it. You were there while I was being formed in utter seclusion! You saw me before I was born and scheduled each day of my life before I began to breathe. Every day was recorded in Your Book!

How precious it is, Lord, to realize that You are thinking about me constantly! I can't even count how many times a day Your thoughts turn towards me. And when I waken in the morning, You are still thinking of me!"

Life Lessons

Laugh from your gut.

Spend your moments in thankfulness.

Be as empty as you can be
when that clock winds down.

Spend your life.

And if time is a river,
MAY YOU LEAVE A WAKE!!!

Books that have greatly influenced
my life and the writing of this booklet:

Bringing Heaven Into Hell – Merlin Carothers
Prison to Praise – Merlin Carothers
(These first two books are about being thankful
and praising God for everything. I highly
recommend them both!)

The Treasure Principle – Randy Alcorn
(This is a short book that teaches the principles of
and the reasons for giving.)

Undone By a Revelation of the Lamb
– Sandy Davis Kirk, Ph.D.
(This book gives a greater revelation of Who Jesus
Christ is and all He has done for you.)

Grace & Forgiveness – John & Carol Arnott
(This is about the importance of forgiving ourselves
and others and how it affects us when we don't.)

Most Inspirational Movie

War Room (2015) – Alex Kendrick, Director

More books by YOLT Publishing

Choices—*Every choice you make has a part in shaping your life for good or for bad. With that in mind, you may want to consider the decisions you make on a daily basis. Ultimately the choices are up to you, so I urge you to choose wisely!*

The Power of a Dream—*This story is about how God brought two totally different people together to change a little piece of the world.*

YOLT Junior: You Only Live Twice—*Don't be afraid to dream big. With God's help you can accomplish great things. Your life matters regardless of your age.*

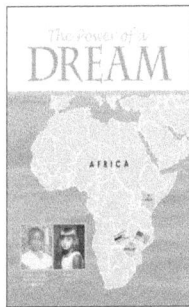

www.YOLTPublishing.com